Dialogues with Jen

Dialogues with Jen

On Issues of Daily Living

Donald R. Fletcher

RESOURCE *Publications* · Eugene, Oregon

DIALOGUES WITH JEN
On Issues of Daily Living

Resource Publications
An Imprint of Wipf and Stock Publishers
199 W. 8th Ave., Suite 3
Eugene, OR 97401

www.wipfandstock.com

PAPERBACK ISBN: 978-1-5326-5107-6
HARDCOVER ISBN: 978-1-5326-5108-3
EBOOK ISBN: 978-1-5326-5109-0

Manufactured in the U.S.A.   SEPTEMBER 17, 2018

To swimmers in life's river,

unwilling just to be swept along

by the current.

Contents

Acknowledgments

As often happens with writers, one book begets another. My *Dialogues with Jay: On Life and Afterlife,* based freely on the pattern of Plato's Dialogues, saw five friends, representing three generations, come together to talk about a major theme. Here they are again, except that Jay, their leader, is replaced by Jennifer—Jen, and that they grapple now with some urgent situations of daily living.

I have drawn on experiences of family and friends, never with personal reference nor details, and on news of the world we all share. My aim is to be relevant, without being personally specific.

In the preparation of this book, as with several previous manuscripts, I have depended on my daughter Sylvia Fletcher, through many hours and days, for suggestions, corrections, and patient help. And, in addition, I have, again, availed myself of the counsel of my literary advisor Roger Williams, of Washington, DC.

Donald R. Fletcher
Lions Gate
Voorhees, New Jersey
April 15, 2018

Dialogue I

I WASN'T SURE I wanted to go in.

Light poured down the front steps and across the drive-way. The windows were full of light, of voices and moving shapes. A couple of the windows, set open, let it spill into the dark, an unusually warm and velvet dark for early October. The whole scene at Luc's house—my long-time friend, Lucas—was bright and welcoming, but I wasn't sure.

"Go on in." That was Jay's voice in my head.

Right! He'd have been glad to be here. I went quickly up the steps.

Inside, there was the noise and bustle of more people than I had expected. Luc's daughter, Beth, was there, of course, and her friend Ian, whom I knew, along with quite a number of their friends. I was looking around for people I knew from my age group when Luc came up, bringing one of the guests.

"Don," he said, "I want you to meet Jen—Jennifer—a younger friend of Jay."

She laughed at the designation. "Not so much younger," she said, "but proud to be associated with his name in any way I can."

She was rather tall, for a woman of her generation, and I was struck by her penetrating gray eyes. When she spoke, her voice was strong, though carefully modulated.

I was happy to chat with Jen—Jennifer. Her name, as she told me, was a Cornish form of the Welsh appellation that became Guinevere. That lent it an aura, and it also was good to know that Jen's friendship with Jay went back quite a few years. It had been only weeks, that evening, since Jay had died, and his strong, serene spirit seemed to be there. I remarked on that, and Jen smiled.

It was about then that Luc rang on his glass with a spoon until all conversation ebbed.

"Beth has a word for us," he said.

Beth stepped forward, with Ian beside her. Her face glowed, and she spoke clearly: "Ian and I want to share with you that we are going to be married. We are working on wedding plans, and you will all receive invitations. But for now, we just want to share our happy news."

There was an immediate din of exclamations, embraces, and all of that. It was later, as people were beginning to leave, that Jen drew me aside.

"I know something about the conversations Jay had with you and Luc, Beth, and Ian. They meant a lot to him. Maybe you'd like to get together again. I'm offering my place—not that I would try to continue where he left off, but to take up other ideas that touch us all. I'd propose a focus on some acute issues of daily living, while keeping, always, a spiritual dimension."

Jen's frank invitation appealed to me.

"Yes," I said. "I'd like that, and I think the others would, too."

"Good." Jen plainly had thought this through. She added, "And for a topic, building on this evening, we might like to reflect on Romantic Love."

That was all at that time, and it was enough. I learned from Luc that Jen lived alone, as a retired middle-school English teacher. Her husband had died rather young, and there were no children. It was three weeks later, on a Sunday afternoon in late October, that the other four of us gathered on the porch of Jen's home. It was distinctly old-style suburban, with a wide porch that ran across the front of the house and down one side. We were glad to go inside as a chill breeze was coming up, and I was pleased to see a couple of small logs—real, home-style firewood—burning in the fieldstone fireplace at one side. There were comfortable chairs, not pre-arranged but easily drawn together.

After a bit of small talk we seemed, all of us, quite content to let some moments of reflective silence float in the late-afternoon sunlight filtering from outside. Then Jen began:

"I'm the new one in this group, and probably we're all thinking of our dear and admired friend Jay; but you've done me the favor of coming to my home, so I'll venture to propose a theme. Actually, I'll reiterate the one Beth and Ian gave us at that delightful gathering when you announced your engagement: what is romantic love, this kind of force between a woman and a man? Let's think about that."

She stopped, seeming ready to let anyone else come in. When none of us did, she went on.

"From a purely physical point of view, one can say that it's a matter of hormones. This is something that happens between a male and a female of our species, a function of the evolution of the reproductive glands that we carry. Luc, as a scientist, probably you can speak best to that."

Luc shrugged, saying, "I'll defer to you. You brought it up, so I'm sure you have further thoughts along that line."

"All right," Jen said. "As a lay person, I'll just start by observing that at the center of survival of any form of life is its reproduction. For a wide range of species, from simple to complex, this means some kind of union, of coming together of female and male, that generally has evolved in a rhythm of ovulation and fertilization. And that's where hormones come in. Such a rhythm, as we move up the scale of complexity, is prompted and controlled by hormones, the chemical substances that reproductive glands secrete.

"I have no expertise to carry that analysis further, and likely don't need to. What I find relevant, as we're talking about romantic love, is that the union of female and male, necessary for procreation, opens up a whole panorama of fascinating behaviors."

"It really does!" That was Beth, breaking in delightedly. "I love the way you put that, about 'fascinating behaviors.' All kinds of animals have their rituals of courtship that sometimes appear outlandish, even comical."

"We humans can be comical enough ourselves, what we will do to attract the other sex," Luc commented dryly.

"Yes, but let's not get personal," Ian said, with an exaggerated gesture.

We all laughed, aware of the pair of lovers among us. Then Jen took up her theme again.

"Each one of us has, or has had, experience with this almost universal impulse. Eros, the Greeks called it, and spun charming, or sometimes frightening, myths of a powerful deity who could also be perverse, like an impulsive child."

I found that inviting. "Right," I said. "With the resurgence of Greek mythology in the European Renaissance, Eros becomes the Cupid figure, with his bow and arrows. He may be chubby in some artistic renderings, a cute and appealing child, but he is dangerous. He can choose arbitrarily the targets of his arrows, but the choice is fateful. If Cupid's arrow hit you, you were in love, no matter what."

"All are fairy stories, whether charming or frightening," Ian said. "There could be magic potions, too. A sip of this, and with the next person of the other sex whom you happen to see, you will fall madly in love. There's a strand of

4

truth, of real-life experience, that runs through such imaginative folklore."

"What was it, Ian?" Beth demanded, with pretended anger. "What had you been drinking when you told me that you loved me?"

"Don't worry," he countered, "there are no magic potions in our world any more. The truth of the folklore is just that we don't, and we can't, calculate love. I know, you hear this or that married man say, 'When I first saw her it was love at first sight'— even 'I knew that was the person I was going to marry.' Women say that, too. But I'd say that it's not a matter of deliberate, rational selection. You may select a person of the other sex as being wonderfully desirable, but you can't make yourself fall deeply in love with that person nor, much less, can you make that person fall in love with you."

"So, what is it, then," Jen asked, "that is operating here? We get back to the sexual impulse. In many forms of life, and taking many patterns, that impulse essentially involves aggressive pursuit by the male and, by the female, passive receptivity. And the behavior moves in cycles. Particularly among the more complex animal species, there is a rhythm established by the sex glands, times when the female is 'in heat' and receptive, and when the male, consequently, is more aggressive than usual, and more competitive with other males. Hunters and, in general, people of the woods know about these things—when is the 'rutting' season for this or that animal."

I offered a comment. "It seems very interesting to me that of the more advanced species on this planet, we are one of a very few, if I have this right, who don't observe a rutting, or mating, season. With *homo sapiens* it's common for males to be perpetually taking notice of females and be perpetually susceptible to sexual arousal."

Jen went on: "What we're talking about, Eros, carnal love, is as old as the evolutionary beginnings of our species and, at the same time, one of the most basic and important drives in our most sophisticated modern societies. Looking back, we can see that the competition, particularly among males, for a chance at procreation has served a basic evolutionary purpose."

As Jen paused, Luc spoke up.

"Right," he said, "Here are some stags in the forest in the rutting season. You see them fighting, butting each other, locking their antlers. Some may be hurt, even killed. Why? It's the season for mating, and the contest is to see which stag can drive the others away and claim the opportunity to mate with the does that are in heat.

"The result? Their fawns will have his genes, genes of the ablest stag. Stretch that across a hundred, a thousand generations, and you begin to see evolution in action, evolving a viable species."

"I like that," Ian said. "And translated into modern society, it means a constant competition and push toward the top. Hormones no doubt are part of the mix; but I'd say that they appear to blend in with much else that human nature and human social traditions add to it."

"That opens up quite a field for thought," I offered, "and perhaps, for the men here, a chance to shift away from the theme of the aggressive, promiscuous male."

"Sure," Jen responded, getting to her feet. "Let's make it a chance for a cup of coffee, or what else that I can offer you."

Beth and Ian followed her toward the kitchen, and soon we were relaxing, enjoying a choice of beverages and of crumpets and the like, set out on the dining room table.

When we had drifted back to the living room and resumed our comfortable chairs, Jen took the lead again.

"I'd like to move now to a different aspect of love. It's part of the physical, certainly, but among us *homo sapiens,* it has a spiritual aspect as well. I mean, choosing a mate. Beth and Ian have done that. You represent our primary resource, and I find this a promising subject to explore."

I spoke up then. "As I left home today to come over here—well, 'home' being the snug apartment that I'm renting—there was a honking and, when I looked up, a V of Canada geese going over. I've heard how these birds often mate for life. I put that into a haiku once, in a happier time. It was on a fall evening, after rain and almost dark, when this pair of geese passed overhead, low, but in silence."

Beth prompted, "And the haiku?"

So, I spoke it:

> "Gray shadows, silent,
> beating damp air, these two geese
> pass, faithful, my love."

"Beautiful," Jen said. "Thank you, Don. Our inquiry brings us unexpected rewards. About choosing a mate, including a mate for life, one might say that the purpose of coupling is procreation. Each species brings its progeny into the world. After that, it's a question of survival, and the parts taken by the male and female mates for the survival of offspring are interesting to observe."

"So, how about an example?" Luc said.

Jen obliged: "All right, consider a clutch of eggs left by a sea turtle, where she has lumbered up a tropical beach and scooped a hollow in the sand. She leaves them there and returns that same night to the sea. It's the sun's warmth that incubates those eggs, and when the hatchlings eventually emerge, it's their instinct that prompts them to wriggle down toward light on the water and, if they escape all predators, to splash into their natural element. They get no maternal care at any point along the way.

"With the sea hawk that has a nest up on a crag, it's a different story. She broods her eggs, and when they hatch she must begin the task of finding and bringing them prey, and tearing it into bits they can swallow. That continues until at long last, after endless squawking and clamoring, the chicks have grown wings that are strong enough for them to leave the nest, mature, find mates, and build nests of their own."

Ian spoke up. "I don't know how it is with sea hawks, but in some bird species the male partner, having done his part to fertilize the eggs as they were forming, stays around and helps to feed and protect the chicks."

Beth joined in, "That's the preferable kind of mate. We mammals have it harder, though. With us, the evolutionary process heaps the whole primary burden on the female. She has to carry the progeny in her body until it can live on its own."

"Until hatched, that is?" Ian put in, with a laugh.

"No," Beth countered. "The mammalian hatchling, if you want to call it that, can't manage outside food. It has to nurse from its mother, or a surrogate mother, until it's more developed. The male may help by foraging for the female, but she has to provide the critical nourishment for the offspring. So instinct varies here. In some mammalian species, the male stays around for protection. In others, he isn't there, not for the birth, nor afterward."

"A human parable." That was Luc, with his dry humor. "Ours is by far the most intelligent and resourceful of the mammalian species, but not the most dependable. Instinct, in us, has been plastered over by layers of civilization. That deadening appears to produce among us a lot of deadbeat dads."

"Sad, but true," Jen rejoined to that, "which shows that for our species, and at the present stage of evolution of our society, the female should take special care in choosing a mate."

She gave that comment whimsical emphasis, with a smile at us three men, so I picked up the thread.

"The choice isn't always so freely made. Even the most primitive society introduces limits and taboos. Generally, less is left to choice and more to custom and tradition. We all know about societies in which marriages are arranged for children, sometimes almost before they learn to walk. And then, there was the era of royal families, in which marriage was a political tool. Now, that seems passé, although the 'marriage of convenience' certainly is still around."

"But how much is really choice?" Jen asked. "Any sizeable group of youthful people sorts itself, by and large, into couples. Is this by ancient evolutionary instinct? It's naturally hormonal for the sexes to gravitate toward each other, but what prompts specific, individual selection? That seems mysterious. To be sure, it doesn't always work. There is the triangle—a framework for sagas of reality as well as fiction—when two members of one sex pursue the same one of the other. And there are other problems, tragedies small and large; but to a remarkable degree, as it seems, when social custom permits it, a spontaneous pairing occurs."

"Right," said Luc, "and that's instinct, left free to operate."

"Well, now," Ian came in, "this could be getting personal. What Beth and I announced the other evening wasn't just a gurgling of hormonal instinct. I hope we see each other as more than that!"

There was a ripple of laughter, with a touch of embarrassment. I felt that I could offer a comment on that.

"Certainly," I said, "here are two highly complex people. Sexual urges are present, and, no doubt, other instinctual promptings. I dare say we've all experienced such. But for human marriage at its best there needs to be a fitting together of two complex beings in many ways.

"Here enters Shakespeare's theme of 'the marriage of true minds,' in his Sonnet 116. Two minds may be very different in their interests, their knowledge, and their skill of thought; but each one needs to bring to their shared life her or his special focus and gifts, and needs to have a full appreciation of what the other brings. Which is to say that neither partner should try to shape the other. Let her be herself, and him be himself. They are unique, even while, living together, they will be building up a single, central home and life."

"I agree with that," Luc said. "But the structure of a shared home and life has to have common ground on which it can be built. The two people need to share a bedrock foundation of life, a basic set of ideas and ideals about living. If they don't have that, they can find themselves pulling in different directions. And if there are children, and Mom is saying, Do this, try to be this; while Dad says, No, not that way, what I'm telling you is better; the kids won't know which way to go. Marriage partners are different—fine—but they must have a common ground to build on."

"The sum of it all," I proposed, "is that these two rich, complex personalities choose to work at fitting themselves together. That's love—conscious, purposeful love."

"Thanks, Don," Beth said, "and Dad, too. That's how Ian and I see it, as we've talked about it. We don't try to be the same. He compensates for me, and I for him. How boring it would be, if we were too much alike! He isn't the dominant male, either. Neither of us intends to dominate, but rather to recognize the qualities that each of us lacks, and that the other brings to our being together. At least, that's how we've said we want it to be. Let's hope we can make it work."

"Well put!" Jen said. "You are two people with similar viewpoints, so that finding the common ground that Luc speaks of probably is natural enough. But at the same time, you are two different people, and there will be moments—crises, perhaps—in which your differences will stand out, stark and plain. You didn't go out to look for and to choose a mate who is different, but your love made the choice. Be able to recognize that—even be glad for it. Make of your differences something to cherish in one another, two quite distinct halves of one complete whole.

"That, I'd say, is love. Eros is part of it, the strong, basic urge. But it is also the human spirit at its finest."

The early winter evening was coming on. Our talk had reached a natural end point, a time for us to rise, find our coats, and, with hearty thanks to our hostess, go out into the brisk, gathering darkness.

Dialogue II

My cell phone vibrated in my pocket. It was Ian.

"Don, my uncle has a cabin in the Poconos. I was telling him about our conversation at Jen's place, and he said, 'If your group wants to get together again, where you can think and talk and not be disturbed, why don't you use my cabin? It's quiet enough up there, and the woods are beautiful, even at this time of year.' I thanked him and said I would consult you."

We worked it out for a Sunday a couple of weeks later, in mid-November. Ian's uncle also offered his van, and we five rode together, in a festive mood. The Poconos, on the Pennsylvania side of the Delaware River, opposite north central New Jersey, are not large mountains, but the land rises enough for a distinct change in the air. It grew clear and crisp. The November sky, beyond bare, white-birch branches, was steel blue. Before we reached the cabin, we came into a region where there had been a light, early snow.

I wondered how comfortable the cabin might be; but didn't need to. Ian had seen to that. When we went in, after stamping some snow off our shoes, there was a fire laid in the fireplace. Ian soon had it crackling cheerfully, throwing warm flickers on our faces. And within minutes, while Jen and I were still admiring the snug cabin and its graceful setting on the brow of a hill, Beth and Ian had coffee and hot apple cider on the white-pine table.

When we were comfortably arranged in a semi-circle facing the fireplace, some with our cups still in hand, and Luc had adjusted the electric heat as well, Jen began.

"What an idyllic location this is! Plato's Socrates could have gladly exchanged his grove of olive trees outside of Athens for the white birches on this hilltop. So, remembering him, we'll let the talk and the ideas flow. At my house several weeks ago we were considering Eros and romantic love, and how two lovers get together. Is it instinct, or choice, or what?"

"I spoke up for instinct," Luc said. "Not that we understand that completely. Instinct involves memory transmitted through genes—in this case, an impulse by which this individual and that one are drawn together, as suited for one another. How does that work? We have quite a bit to learn before we comprehend it."

"Genes—all right." Now it was Ian. "Traits are inherited. We can mate fruit flies selectively and show how Mendel's laws of heredity work; but this is much more complicated and more subtle. Beth and I, since we seem to get pushed forward here, aren't fruit flies."

Jen laughed. "To be sure," she said lightly, "which is why I brought up this kind of attraction. It has to do with the sexual impulse that we share with many forms of life on this planet, up and down the evolutionary scale. We discussed that in our last conversation. But there seems to be another dimension."

"Call it spirit," I said, glad to interject a comment. "The terms we use for it can tilt our talk toward this or that religious tradition, but I don't think we came up here to discuss religion."

"No, please," Luc protested. "I've been through enough arguments of that kind in my time."

"Then we'll just observe," I went on, "as you and I have talked about it, Luc: that somehow in human evolution, far back along the line, our species began to evolve consciousness, self-awareness. It's quite true that some others of the more intelligent animal species seem to show glimmers of it."

"Yes," Beth broke in, "I've seen that! There's the experiment of having a chimpanzee look at itself in a mirror. The mirror is taken away and a mark, like a colored dot, is stuck to the chimp's face, perhaps above one eye, while other parts of the face are touched as well, as a distraction. When the mirror is brought back, the chimp sees that reflected face again, notices the spot and puts his hand up to the place on his own face to touch it. This is simple self-awareness. Seeing the animal in the mirror, he is to some degree aware that that animal is himself."

"So, gradually," Luc put in, "along the last million years or so of evolutionary development, the various hominid species have acquired and elaborated that awareness."

"Why not?" I challenged, "It's now what sets *homo sapiens,* the only surviving hominid species, widely apart from all other species on the planet. A newborn human child begins early to show consciousness. Quite early, she or he begins to assert self."

"Don't other animals assert themselves?" Beth asked.

"Of course they do," Luc said rather sharply, "in the constant competition to survive. I don't think we're different. Our big brain is just far out ahead of the rest."

I responded to that, "The difference seems to be more than quantitative. I think there is a different quality here. Presumably it has appeared in the course of the evolutionary millennia. When and how, who can reasonably say? What matters is the present reality."

"And how do you define that reality?" Luc's challenge was pointed.

I answered, "For definitions we have to use concrete words. We have to say that a thing consists of this or that substance, or that it functions in this or that way, having this or that effect. Now, what we're talking about may perform, or have historically performed, in ways to produce particular effects, but I can't see that it's susceptible to any definition."

"Then is there any use in trying to say more about it?" Beth wondered. "Dad spoke about the emergence of awareness across the eons of evolution, but apparently, we can't define it now, or say what it really is."

Ian joined in: "I, for one, am better satisfied to consider how this quality, or entity, shows itself in human life, than to try to say what it is."

"So, what might be a first showing?" Luc's tone now had a sarcastic edge.

Ian responded, with a smile, "For Beth and me, that could be easy. What about love?"

"An interesting proposal."

That was Jen's voice, its contralto timbre resounding, just as a log shifted in the fireplace, with a shower of sparks. "Our theme of romantic love fits well here. In our former discussion, we talked about mating by many forms of life, but the experience of love seems qualitatively unique to our species."

"I agree," Beth said, while Ian looked surprised. "Sure, animals show affection; our pets, especially, often seem to show such feelings, and people may call it love; but is it love?"

"Now, Beth," Ian said, "when Roland looks up at you with those soulful, big, brown eyes, how can you say he doesn't simply adore you?"

"Adore?" she answered, "No, definitely not, in the sense we usually give to that word."

Turning to the others, Beth said, "For those who don't know him, Roland is my golden retriever. In Roland's canine world-system I'm the chief human figure. I feed, stroke, and watch over him; so he, in turn, follows, obeys, and protects me. And he wants to be with me, to guard but also to nuzzle and be near.

"Is this love? Is he showing emotion? We know it's easy to attribute human feelings to creatures—objects, even—that aren't human. I'm sure you've taught about that, Jen."

"Oh yes," Jen said, "the 'pathetic fallacy'—'pathetic', from the Greek *pathos,* emotion, feeling. Poets love it, surrounding us with shrieking winds, weeping flowers, and the like."

"Well," Beth continued, "I'm very fond of Roland. I'd say that I love my dog, in one use of the word; but I don't say that he loves, much less adores, me."

"Hmm." That was Ian's comment.

"Right enough," Luc said. "Let the dog be a dog."

Jen returned to the discussion. "Let's say that the human experience that we call love requires, as its object, a being that is able to show love in return. That loved one may not return the love, or only very little, so that the experience is painful for the one whose love is rebuffed; but she or he has to know that there could be love in return."

Now I spoke up. "Are you saying that there can't be love that is completely one sided?"

"Yes," Jen replied, "I think I'd say that. We use the word love loosely, of course; but for the genuine emotional experience I'd say that there has to be at least a hint of possibility of response. Otherwise, what might be thought of as love is simply longing—a wish, maybe very intense, but still just a wish for love. It isn't the experience itself, which has to be two-sided, a meeting of two emotional beings."

"Perhaps," I proposed, "something like this is our best way of getting at a definition of human consciousness, which I would call spirit. That, and only that, comes into play when we feel love. I'm not confining this to romantic love. I'm thinking of any emotional experience in which a person reaches out to another person or people, giving of self, in order to receive from that other self, or selves. Spirit is meeting spirit."

Luc stood up and stretched. "Don is opening up a whole new vista," he said. "From way back in our student days, I know that he likes to do that."

"Well then," Jen said, also getting to her feet, "let's take a break, but remember to come back to Don's point."

"As I remember, there's a pond just down the slope," Beth said. "I don't suppose that any ducks are still around."

"Let's go and see," Jen replied, taking her jacket from one of the wall pegs by the door.

We followed her and were soon tramping through the woods, brushing branches that held light snow. The pond, when we came to it, showed a skin of ice around the edges, with no ducks in sight. But the air was brisk and the sun, down in the southwest, still bright.

A half-hour later we were back in the cabin, with Ian refreshing the smoldering fire. Luc had brought a crock-pot of pulled chicken in barbecue sauce, a specialty of his, and had plugged it in ahead of time, so that when he lifted the lid now, the savory aroma was irresistible. There were large, crispy rolls to split open and toast on long forks at the fire. These, along with tea or coffee, and cold cola or beer, completed the meal. We all felt snug and content, ready to continue our discussion.

I started. "Our physical or animal selves are now satisfied. We've had some exercise, been out in the natural world, and been warmed and fed."

"So, it must be nap time," Luc said, feigning a big yawn, and we all laughed.

"It could be," I went on, "but we are happily conscious of one another. Not only are there warm bodies here of the same species; there are also spirits. There is a possibility of mind engaging mind. With language, humanity's invention, we can form ideas and we can share them. We can load those ideas with emotion, feeling, and convey something of that emotion to one another. What a remarkable, uniquely human phenomenon!

"And it all happens in the physical brain. Damage that brain physically, and it can't happen. But there is a spiritual dimension. There is a quality here that shares, communicates, goes out from spirit to spirit, the unique, irreproducible self that each one is."

I stopped, and there was a long pause. Who could say yes, or no, to that? It was Jen who tried. "Don, I agree. We put words together, trying to give shape to our ideas, our personal insights, and put them out there for others to see and feel, to receive or to push away, and, if received, maybe to add something and put them out again. Each brain is working here, each complete thought-system.

"The brain may be trained to be objective, to be scientifically impartial, looking for what is factual, subject to observation and proof, and only that. But even the scientist is a human self. He or she leaves the lab and goes home to experience or long for love, for the simple, heartening interchange with other selves with whom that self has bonded."

Ian had been sitting near the fireplace, looking into the fire. Now he spoke. "You are speaking my language. It's a figurative language, all conveyed in pictures, because it doesn't talk about objects, about things in the outside world, about what happens, or can be made to happen, to them. It talks about the inner self, the conscious self, and what that self experiences. One of the simplest, and most notable, of such experiences, I think, is music.

"Our planet world has always been full of sounds, and many forms of life have evolved organs of hearing, able to distinguish sounds and respond appropriately—maybe for food or flight. A good many species have evolved means of producing sound—by rubbing legs or wings together, or by forcing air through an organ of sound."

"Is that what you go to a concert for," Beth demanded of him, "to hear air forced through an organ of sound?"

"Why not?" Ian answered, unfazed. "If you enjoy hearing it, why not? And to keep my train of thought on track, let me point out that humanity, as it *became* humanity, was learning to sound words at different pitches and to arrange those pitches in different sequences that could have a variety of meanings; or, at least, we may conjecture that the development had some such pattern."

"What about the tie to music you mentioned?" Luc asked.

"Coming momentarily," Ian responded. "Some humans began to find certain pitches, and certain sequences of such pitches, pleasing. I'll leave to the specialists in music theory—maybe some of you—to explain tonal sequence, and how it is that in various parts of the world ethnic groups have developed their musical traditions according to distinct tonal patterns that they have found pleasing and expressive.

"So, what is the conclusion, the terminal at which I hope that my train of thought has arrived? It is that humanity's music, in all its wonderfully rich variety, is a direct expression of the human spirit. Many living species communicate their necessities by making sounds, but human music goes far beyond that. It is an expression of, by, and for the human spirit."

Beth started to speak but checked herself. Instead, as she was not close enough to touch Ian, she gave him a smiling thumbs-up. I was glad to add a word. "Fine, Ian," I said. "We've all enjoyed the ride on your thought-train, right to the terminal. The variety and complexity of music, from as early as we have any inkling of human thought, is an expression of spirituality. It brings up a related idea, which is inspiration."

Now Beth's voice did come in. "I have a friend who is a composer, writing music mostly in a classical style. She was telling me how she had a commission to write a piano concerto. Its premiere performance had been scheduled, and the date was approaching. She had to get something on paper, and get it into the hands of the solo pianist and the orchestra, but no ideas would come and she began to panic. She was about to say, with total chagrin, that the concert premiere would have to be postponed, when one morning she woke up and the plan of the entire concerto was in her mind. Within five days she had written out in full the long first movement, with the other two movements already sounding in her mind, ready to be elaborated.

"Where did it come from? She could only smile and shrug, with open palms."

Saying that, Beth made the gesture.

"That's right," Jen said, from her end of the semicircle we had formed at a comfortable distance from the fireplace. "Artists say that it is inspiration—etymologically, a breath or air blowing in. What they're expressing, in whatever words, is a sense that their creative impulse is not something that they can deliberately induce or control. The working out of it may be done quite methodically; but the initial design, the artistic concept, has seemed to come from outside their rational thought, as if breathed into them from a mysterious source. That's inspiration."

"And what about the rest of us," Luc wanted to know, "most of humanity, who aren't creative artists, whatever the medium?"

"I think there can be inspiration," I offered, "in many phases of human experience. I'd say that the human spirit may sense and respond to such impulses in unexpected times and ways."

"Which come from where, by what kind of act, or will?"

That was Ian, turning his face again toward the fire and sending the question out into the room, not as a challenge, but as a perennial, unanswered quest. We let it hover there, no one offering a reply.

After a bit of silence, I said. "The where of inspiration is probably not a *where* at all. Being spiritual—of spirit—it doesn't belong to space/time reality, but is transcendent."

As I paused, Beth queried me. "Transcendent—what does that mean in this context?"

"What it means to me, at least," I said, "is that in speaking of spirit we are crossing a boundary, going out of the factual world of time and space. Everything we can observe and know in this universe is temporal and spatial. As such, it can be measured and calculated, and can be established as fact—factual reality. Spirit, the spiritual, is not so. Is it therefore unreal?

"Yes, if we limit ourselves to factual reality. But if we go beyond that reality, if we let our human spirit move free of the limits of space and time, we are transcending those limits. Our human spirit is demonstrating—maybe falteringly and imperfectly but nonetheless demonstrating—that it is transcendent. It is able to break out of factual reality, to share somewhat, somehow, in a transcendent reality."

I stopped, seeming to hear an echo of my own voice, and feeling abashed that I had used such large, incalculable words. The room was silent. A burned-through log in the fireplace collapsed, with a soft thud and a flurry of sparks, and in that moment a clock in the hallway struck four.

Jen spoke. "Don, you've opened a very wide vista, giving us plenty to reflect on; but we have a couple of hours of road time until we reach our homes. Probably we should be leaving this cabin, with special thanks to Ian for arranging for it, and to Luc and Beth for feeding us so well, and be on our way."

It felt good to be getting to our feet, and soon we were gathering up and going out to the low winter sunlight, where it slanted through a screen of bare branches. Ian checked his list, to be sure that the cabin was left secure, then slid behind the wheel of the van. The tires crunched, and we were on the road.

DIALOGUE III

WE WERE OCCUPIED IN our various ways over Thanksgiving, Christmas, New Year's, and whatever winter holidays each one had. I'd received an assignment to write a series of articles and was absorbed by that for some weeks. Then, in early February, Jen sent an email to the other four of us.

"Hi, All of You. I have a vacation house at the Jersey shore. How about getting together down there on Saturday, the twenty-first, around 11:00 am? I'll send along the address, and there's a good pizzeria nearby for lunch."

We all liked the idea, and Beth added, "I know Roland would like to come, too, if that's okay. He enjoys the beach, summer or winter."

On the twenty-first, we arrived right on time. I rode with Luc, and Ian's van pulled up just ahead of us, with Roland jumping out first. It was a bright day, with a brisk breeze blowing in off the ocean. Jen came out on the white porch of her house, holding close the jacket she had thrown around her shoulders.

Inside, the air was warm and inviting. Jen had coffee ready, hot water for tea, and some tempting Danish and gingerbread. We were just a block from the ocean. When I cracked the door open to listen, I could hear the surf.

It took a while, of course, for the exclamations and pleasantries. At length we were settled in a comfortable, casual circle that Jen had arranged, and she began. "We aren't a committee and don't need a leader, but since you kindly took up my suggestion to gather here at my vacation house— winter vacation, today—I'll offer a topic. I think it follows naturally from our talk, back in the fall, about romantic love.

"I'm thinking back a good many years, to my elder sister, Edna, when we were both young. She was engaged to be married. Our parents didn't know the young man well. In fact, our mother wondered quite openly whether Edna knew him that well, either. Edna had gotten engaged, and wedding plans were being made. Then, abruptly, she announced that she was going to Paris with a girlfriend. She was old enough, certainly, to make her own decisions. But what about her fiancé and the wedding? They even had the invitations ready to send out.

"'No wedding,' Edna said, 'I'm not going to do it.' She went off to Paris, and by the time she came back with Ella, her girlfriend, she told our parents that *they* were going to live together.

"Remember, this was quite a while back, maybe forty-five years ago. Most people didn't talk openly, yet, about lesbian couples. Edna did have a long talk with our mom and dad. She told them how she had realized, as her wedding was coming close, that it wasn't right for her. She couldn't do it. And then, when she went away with Ella, she began to realize that Ella was more than a close girlfriend. This was the person, the one person in all the world, whom she deeply loved."

Jen stopped. There was a long silence. We could hear the breeze blowing through the well-secured shutters.

"Did they stay together?" Beth finally asked.

"Yes," Jen said, "until five years ago, when Edna died of ovarian cancer. It was quite soon after that, that Ella, driving alone at night, apparently lost control of her car and smashed into an overpass abutment. The autopsy showed no trace of alcohol or drugs, and we were left wondering. Did she really lose control? The state trooper who came on the wreck, on that isolated stretch of road, reported that there were no skid marks and that her seat belt had not been fastened."

Again, there was a silence in our circle. I felt, almost, that those two spirits and their deep and long love were with us there.

At length Beth spoke. "Theirs was romantic love, as total and compelling as any love can be."

"Romantic love," I said, "can sometimes bring together people of very different backgrounds and traditions—even of quite opposite personalities."

"What draws people together, when they seem very unlike?" Beth wondered. "Dad, is that your instinct, underneath?"

Luc said, "Probably it is. The partners, in such couples, may not really be so different. There may be an instinctual affinity at work, all the time—genes in each one tugging toward the other. This force is maybe more obvious with simple physiological differences: tall men attracted to small, even petite women, or large, burley men to delicate, seemingly fragile women, and vice versa. It's the kind of force that helped us in our evolutionary development."

"Now that's an appealing thought," Ian said. "Cupid dips his arrows in our genetic broth. His aim sometimes seems random, but the effect is sure. Genes respond to genes. Romantically, we're just acting out a script already written for us in the tiny dots on the double helix of one of our twenty-three chromosomes."

Beth broke in, "Ian, if that's the way you see it, I don't. I choose to love; I don't just have to. I tell myself that I could get along without you."

"Oh, do you? Then what if I let you try it?"

Ian was busy keeping a tone of playful banter; but there was an edge. Roland lifted his head from between his paws to look at him, and Jen stepped in.

"Come now, you two," she said. "We trust your genes, and we trust your mature sense of each other, too. You know who you are, and how right it is for you to be together. We all value that and we love you for it."

She paused, and Roland gave his tail a couple of wags, thumping the floor.

I said, "I think Roland wants to reassure us all. Maybe we need to ponder these things, having a walk on the beach while the sun is high. Roland will certainly approve of that."

"I'm for it," Luc responded, getting up. "The beach can be great at this time of year."

Within minutes we were bundled up, scarves, gloves, and all, and our breath steamed as we jostled down the block to where the pavement ended. The first sand was dry; the going loose and uneven. Then, where the tide reached when it was high, the waves had packed the beach firm. Roland took off at a long lope, with Beth and Ian after him. We older three followed at a brisk walk, inhaling the sharp, salty air. The sea was coming ashore in a modest froth of breakers, and beyond them the horizon was drawn across, straight and clear. We stopped to look toward it, and to feel the wind, and the high bowl of gray and blue atmosphere that enclosed us.

"I love the beach," Jen was saying. "I love it in the summer, with people playing, swimming, dozing, all drenched in sunlight. But I think I almost love it more like this—so plain, wide-open, just elemental."

"That's the way it makes me feel, as well," Luc said. "Right here, now, everything civilized is built on the land behind us; but, facing out, we have ocean and sky, as they've been since long before there were any human eyes to see them."

I nodded, content to feel the scene, as well as see it, without looking in my head for words.

After a bit we gathered again at the end of our street. Then, back at Jen's house, we got in our cars to ride the three or four blocks to the pizzeria that Jen had talked about, finding it brightly painted and congenial, and the pizza very good.

So, in a short while, we were once more in our circle in Jen's living room. Clouds had rolled in off the ocean. Because we were now quiet, I could hear the surf, muffled but more distinct than before. I expected that it would again be Jen who would take the lead; instead, it was Luc.

"Out there on the beach today, I felt I wanted to share something personal, something really between Beth and me. So I asked Beth a few minutes ago, and she agreed.

"Fifteen years ago my marriage to Marian came to an end. How much more you know doesn't matter. I bring it up, because we have been talking about romantic love, how that bond forms, usually between a woman and a man. Marian and I formed ours when we were still quite young; but we felt sure of it.

"The crisis came when Beth was twelve, as she knew only too well. Marian left. Some of my friends heard, afterward, that she was in another relationship. How much more they heard, or knew, I can't say. Beth wasn't a young child; but we didn't talk about it. I knew that she cried a lot, and that it hurt her very much. I tried, but couldn't really comfort her.

"It was about two years after the separation that I heard that Marian was ill. How ill, I didn't know—until the word came that she was gone. Marian had kept in touch with Beth, but had said nothing about her illness.

"Why talk about this now? Because there was a scene, burned in my memory, that I need to share, of how love can take a strange and perhaps twisted form. Of course, I told

Beth about it, when she grew older. Now I share it, but just in this private, confidential circle.

"There was this friend who came into our lives—I'm not going to mention his name. I knew him only moderately well; I was traveling at that time. Marian got to know him, shall we say, much better. I was aware of that—aware enough to ask her, one day, about her feelings. I see her yet, her face distorted by the force of her emotion, crying out:

"'I love him. You need to know that. But I love you, too; I always have. How can I love two men at the same time, in the same way? How can I? How can that be?'

"In spite of the shock, I felt completely calm. I said to her, 'You have to choose. There can't be two of us. You have to decide.'

"My work made me go away for two days, and when I came back, Marian had left. That was all."

Luc's voice had seemed to fill the room. Now it stopped, but the story and its characters hung in the air—especially Marian, and her tortured question. Ian went over and knelt, putting his arm around Beth, as she covered her face with her hands.

"I'm sorry, dear Beth," Luc said. "It still hurts—hurts both of us." Then he went on, to the rest of us, "In the divorce court Marian made a try for custody."

Beth looked up and spoke, her voice strong and clear. "The judge listened to Mom's lawyer, and then he turned to me. 'You are quite old enough to understand and to make up your mind,' he said. 'What would you choose to do?'"

Beth paused, then took a slow breath and went on. "Mom had cut deep into our relationship and the love I had for her. I didn't hesitate. I said, 'I'll stay with my dad.'"

Again, our room went quiet. After a little, I said, "How amazing—how literally, fearfully amazing! Love is the highest—and the most powerful—emotional force that we know."

Jen said, "We'll accept it at that. We're grateful, Luc, for what you shared with us, and that you chose this time and place to share it. Your trust is safe with us; we will hold sacred that scene, and Marian's decision, however it may appear to each one of us. And Beth, our hearts are open to you, without being able to know what you have felt about your mother and may now feel. I simply want to say that our circle has been drawn close. We will ponder, Luc, what you've entrusted to us all."

Ian stood and went back to his chair, speaking as he went. "I'm grateful for the insight you've given me. I know it will deepen Beth's and my relationship."

"Love often requires painful choices," Jen said. "Romantic love commonly means leaving home, one's parental home; and the break may be greater than that—leaving one's entire social setting, possibly one's country. Or love may mean the choice of a whole new direction in one's life, giving up cherished plans and goals to accommodate another person's plans and goals, or to adopt some different, middle course.

"Society—even our 'enlightened' Western society—thought until quite recently that the woman had to conform to the preference and the ambition of the man. That's changing, moving in the direction of equal partnership as a team. There are husbands who can acknowledge that their wives are co-equal in their relationship. Love still needs to make the choice."

"And if the choice of love is painful," I proposed, "it's important for that love not to be so self-absorbed that it fails to sense the pain its choice may cause for others. I won't judge Marian's choice. I have no way to know how hard it was for her to make, nor what compelling need she may have had.

"But she had to have known, very well, the pain it would inflict on the two people she was leaving. The choices that love makes—those that may be for joy, as well as pain—spill over into other people's lives."

Now Beth spoke: "I can say yes to that. And I hope that the joy that Ian and I have come to feel may spill over into many lives, now, and in years to come."

"May it be so," Luc said. "You deserve all the joy you may find, my dear."

There was more discussion along those lines, but I felt that what was essential had been said.

After a while, Jen wrapped it up, saying, "Maybe we've reached a good pausing place in our conversation. I'm glad that you accepted my invitation to a winter's day at the shore. Oh yes, and that Roland came along. I hope there may be another place and time."

Dialogue IV

THE WEEKS SLIPPED BY. It was early April when an email message got our dialogue group together again. This time the message was from Luc. He wrote that a friend had a modest but comfortable place in the Pine Barrens where he liked to withdraw from time to time to be quiet and quite alone—his hermitage, he called it. The friend wouldn't be there for a while, and we were welcome to use the place. Luc proposed Saturday, the fifteenth of the month. By the evening of the day his message arrived we had all agreed on the place and date.

New Jersey's Pine Barrens make up a large tract of land, in the central and southern part of the state, that is too sandy for agriculture. The Barrens are actually not barren; in places they are wooded, quite densely, mostly with a dwarf pine that can survive in the nutrient-poor soil. Historically, the region has been scantily populated, and it is now set aside as a strictly controlled reserve.

When our day came, we made our way by a dirt road a mile or two past one boundary of the reserve and pulled up at Luc's friend's "hermitage." It was a small frame house with white clapboard, tidily maintained. A border of better soil surrounded the front, and in the April sunshine crocuses were blooming.

The few rooms, all neatly kept, were quickly explored. I had brought lunch supplies which I stowed in the kitchen. We made a circle of a loveseat and three large chairs in the front room. As one would expect, Ian and Beth took the loveseat, with Roland occupying a braided rug at their feet. Beth was obviously tense. Jen started us off with a few welcoming words, and then Beth broke out:

"How could they do it? How could anyone do it? This was their child!" She ended with a shudder.

Luc responded, "No, my dear, not a child, not yet. This was a fetus, still in formation—and malformation, as it seems."

"I say it was a child—*their* child," Beth retorted. "And I don't see how they, or anyone, could do that."

Ian turned to Jen and me to explain. "On the way down, Beth was texting friends of ours, Claire and John, who got married last year. Claire was pregnant, and she'd told Beth that she was far enough along to go for a screening. So we were waiting to hear about that. And just before we got here, Claire texted that the report wasn't good: there was clear evidence of Down syndrome."

"Down syndrome!" Beth burst in. "That isn't fatal!"

There was a momentary, tense silence.

"And so?" Jen prompted, though we could all guess the "so."

"So they terminated the pregnancy," Ian said.

Now the silence was so complete we could hear a clock ticking in the hallway. Jen had opened a window. There was enough breeze to stir the curtains, a pleasant breath of woods, of a recent shower, and sun. That contrasted sharply with the mood that had abruptly filled the room.

Then Beth said more slowly, as if asking herself, "Why would they do that? So, the child would need care—special love and care; but they could give that."

"The child could need a *lot* of care," Luc said, "with maybe some disfigurement, mood problems, seizures, and very limited brain development."

"I know that," Beth retorted, "but this is a person."

"Not yet," Luc said, "and not now."

Ian came in, "It's hard for me to put myself in their place, although I know that Beth and I could be, some time. From the outside, I'm tempted to think of it as a selfish choice. Accepting the birth could mean accepting years of strain—physical, financial, social, emotional strain. No one easily chooses that. But do you say no to your own flesh—no to your life and love together?"

Jen spoke. "I knew Claire as a student, quite a few years ago. She was bright and very personable, outstanding. I remember once, though, when I had given her a lower grade than she thought that she deserved. Her mother came to see me, which was very unusual in junior high school, and told me, in effect, that Claire was used to having things go her way.

"I can understand that in this experience, now, she found herself facing a prospect that was not at all as she proposed her life to be. And there was a way out . . . so she chose it."

Ian responded, "I say it wasn't just Claire. Sure, she's the one who would have to go through the pregnancy and childbirth; but what about John? If he were going to be a good father, he'd need to shoulder a large share of the burden of extra-difficult childcare, of time given, of patience, of ignoring stares and unwelcome pity and all of that, when he'd planned for things to be so different. I'm supposing that John agreed to the termination. Maybe he even urged it. I'm not letting him off the hook."

I had something to say. "Along the line of our recent discussion, the dilemma faced by Claire and John is one of love's dilemmas. I can't know how painful it was, is, and possibly will be for them, and I won't pass judgment on their choice. I hope that it was made by both of them, together, out of love.

"In situations like this, the mind does its work, considering carefully the possibilities, and how each contingency might be met. But fundamentally, as I see it, the choice that is made is spiritual—of the human spirit. Down syndrome is quite physical, Luc; not so?"

As I turned to him, Luc said, "Exactly. A genetic roll of the dice—an extra chromosome, or part of one, that is apparently left in the nucleus of the fertilized egg. It keeps copying itself in every multiplying cell. There's no hostile agent here, as far as is known—just a random occurrence. Perhaps, in time, we will learn to offset it."

"In our present context," I answered, "the offsetting needs to be of the spirit. The discoveries of genetics are marvelous, the why and how of inherited factors, favorable and unfavorable. The genes we carry go together to constitute, in large part, our life, the individual person that each one is. They influence the complex functioning of the brain, and what your brain is and does is who you are.

"So, that's all? I believe not. That word 'believe' is important. It's not a scientific word, because we're moving into a different realm, where scientific method doesn't apply. The human spirit is not scientifically quantifiable. It can't be taken apart and analyzed. What it does—the effects that it has in personal behavior and in society—are certainly to be observed and discussed. Such aspects are real enough; but the essential being I'm referring to, using the word 'spirit', is of a reality that can't be described in the space/time language of this cosmos. Is it, then, an 'airy nothing'? Is it unreal? It is not part of observable, space/time reality. Then, how do we know that it exists? Those of us who know,

know by our awareness. We are aware of a spiritual reality. In fact, we affirm it as transcendent, ultimate reality. Reversing a scientific bias, we declare a conviction that space and time—the present universe around us—is provisional. For all its vastness, it is limited. As reality, it is not necessarily the only or the final reality."

I stopped, then said, "Maybe that's enough, and we need a break"; but Jen said, "No, go on; finish your argument." So I continued.

"The share that each of us has in spiritual reality is our personhood, our existence as that unique human individual that each one is. This is something that develops and changes. In a human infant, we watch with fascination as it begins to emerge, and we may remark on inherited traits—how he or she is just like this or that parent or grandparent in temperament or behavior. Of course, personality is complex, and is influenced by society and environment in many ways.

"What I am saying is that spirit has its own reality—its own being—and that being appears to transcend present, space/time existence. Does spirit, then, come from beyond—and go on beyond—our present life? We don't and can't *know,* in a sense of observable, scientific knowledge. We will have our individual speculations or convictions, which will be matters of belief, articles of faith.

"The sum of my argument is this: every decision that affects our life has a spiritual dimension, because we are spiritual beings. Claire and John's decision is having, and is going to have, a profound effect on each of them individually—on each one's spirit—and on their life together, their relationship, their love. In addition, they are likely to bear, perhaps suffer—consciously or not—the presence of that other spirit that they chose not to include in their life together."

"I think that sounds frightening," Beth said.

"I don't mean it to be," I answered. "Mysterious, yes; there's always something of mystery around spirit, because precise language of analysis doesn't apply. But I don't mean to conjure up any notion of a vindictive ghost."

Jen came in on that. "Don, what you've outlined about spiritual being resonates fully with me. And because our present life is fitted into time and place, we think that way. We think of a 'where' to which we may 'go' as spirit, after death, and also, maybe, from which we come, as spirit, at the time of our birth. Maybe you would say that's inadequate, at best, because it's using space/time language and way of thinking to try to reach outside of space and time."

"No use in trying," Ian proposed. "We can trace the gradual, physical formation of a human in the uterus, but what about the spirit? Is that taking shape—that thing or quality that has no shape? The manifestation of human spirit, it seems, is consciousness, awareness of self. The newborn human infant shows no sign of it. It only begins to appear months after birth, and then it has a long growth process on its way to achieving reasonable maturity as a person."

"So," Luc said pointedly, "what are you saying that re-lates to Claire's decision, with or without John, to terminate her pregnancy?"

That brought a pause. Who would reply? After a brief silence, Ian made a try.

"I think we are saying, or at least I am, that their choice, in physical terms, is not to proceed with a developing fetus. That fetus, being human, brings in a spiritual perspective. But we don't have spiritual knowledge. We don't even have tools of language or thought-form for conceiving adequate-ly of spiritual being. We can only conjecture as to a spiritual effect of that physical termination. If spirit transcends time, it isn't subject to time. Then, possibly, it isn't meaningful to think of a decision such as this one as denying a life to a person who should have had one. I know—it's easy to lose ourselves in useless speculation. We don't know—we don't have the tools to know—and likely it's well, for now, that we don't."

There was, again, reflective silence in the room. After a few moments, Jen said, "Who's ready for a tramp in the 'barren' woods?"

We all quickly donned jackets, hats, and sunglasses, then followed Roland's waving tail along a trail that led, up a long, gradual slope, to a metal-frame fire-lookout tower. No warden was in sight, and the tower was locked; but we were able to ascend one flight of iron steps and get a view out across several waves of scrub forest. It was good to breathe the spring air and to let the brain change its focus.

When we got back to the house, I brought out my modest luncheon fare, and we shared a meal made more congenial by ginger ale, wine, and a craft beer I had discovered the previous weekend.

After lunch was cleared and stowed, we gathered again in our circle and Jen took up the previous line of thought. "Society takes responsibility for the protection and defense of each individual, even the newborn. There are bitter disputes over the rights of the *unborn,* but we won't get into that now. In terms of spirit, I, for one, am content to acknowledge that we find ourselves at a boundary. Space/time language and modes of thinking are not adequate to go beyond it. Our human spirit tends to affirm a spiritual existence that overlaps—and surpasses—the physical universe.

"According to the oldest evidence we have, humanity, from the beginnings of civilization, has formed ideas of invisible spiritual beings that inhabit and control natural phenomena—sun and rain, lightning and wildfire. Such ideas, as well as the far more advanced teachings of later religious traditions, can be regarded as simply representing a human need. We are confronted by forces and situations that we can't control. And so we cry out to the heavens, to some invisible, superior power, to help us."

Jen paused, and I filled the void. "I think that to acknowledge a reality of the human spirit means, implicitly, to declare faith in a superior spirit or spirits, a wider spiritual reality, which in some traditions has led to belief in a single supreme Spirit. We're trying to cast our thoughts beyond the boundary, and we recognized earlier that our language and thought-forms stop there. Jay once reminded us of the admonition, in the Hebrew scriptures, of Ancient Israel's Prophet of the Exile:

> For my thoughts are not your thoughts,
> nor are your ways my ways,
> says the LORD.
> For as the heavens are higher than the earth,
> so are my ways higher than your ways,
> and my thoughts than your thoughts.
> Isaiah 55:8,9 (NRSV)

"It's well to hold firmly to faith in the reality of spirit, and in the supreme reality of the transcendent Spirit, God. It's well, also, to be very restrained in saying that God wills this or does that. Our ways and thoughts are not God's thoughts and ways."

"So, what does that say about Claire and John's decision?" Beth wanted to know. "Aren't they refusing—I won't say taking away—a life that God was giving them?"

Ian answered: "For me, it says that our thoughts, and our ways of judging, are too limited to comprehend all that is involved here. We can't discern the will and purpose of God. We affirm our faith that God's love is supreme. Claire and John's choice may not have blocked a purpose of God."

Jen said, "I think it would be too glib to say that God's love will make it all come out well. God's love, as I believe, often includes for us a good deal of pain and regret, of wishing we could do over the things that we have done. It's enough, I believe, that God's love doesn't stop us from making serious mistakes—even what appear to be catastrophic mistakes. But I also believe that Love does not abandon us, but is near to help us heal and learn, and to grow toward what we can be."

Jen stopped, and Beth went over to take her hands. Jen responded by hugging Beth. I felt moisture in my eyes, as we all stood.

"That was a beautiful, and timely, closing," I said. "We're grateful to your friend, Luc, for the use of his quiet, serene retreat and to you for bringing us here." There was a special warmth, I thought, in our goodbyes.

DIALOGUE V

It was a Sunday morning in early May when my cell phone announced itself with its several brief tones. When I looked I saw that the caller was Ian.

"Hello," I said, "we're all looking forward to getting together with you and Beth next Sunday at that same pond in the woods, where we gathered last year when Jay was with us."

"That's right, Don," Ian said, "but there's a change. Maybe you've seen this morning's paper. There's an article about an accident late Friday night on Route 92, a drunk driver hitting head-on a couple going home after the high school prom."

"Yes," I answered. "I just opened the paper to the story. Very sad, and what a waste!"

Ian said, "That girl was my sister."

The room rocked around me, and my hand clenched on the phone.

"Ian! How dreadful!"

"My kid sister, Alice." Ian's voice was very steady. "I need to help my mom and dad get through this."

"Of course you do," I responded, "and we'll put aside our group date at the pond."

"No," Ian went on, "that's why I'm calling you. I wanted you to know about Alice, before you read or heard more;

40

but also to say that my parents wish to have a simple and quiet funeral this week, doing it jointly with Dave's parents—the two families for their two children, together. I'll be with them to help them through that.

"But then, next Sunday afternoon, Beth and I want to keep the date with Jen, Luc, and you. I feel a bit numb now, and I feel the need to talk with all four of you, to process my thoughts and feelings."

That was where and how he left it. Sunday came, bright, warm, and beautiful. Luc picked up Jen and me, and we left his car at the edge of the woods. By the time we came down the path, catching a glint of the pond through the trees, we could hear Beth and Ian there, setting up.

It felt strange, for a moment, being in that spot, with the woods, the lapping pond waters, even the daffodils bending in the breeze, exactly as a year ago, but Jay not there with us. The thought passed over. It was Jen with us now. The tragedy in Ian's family had a sobering effect, and it also seemed to draw us closer together. We arranged ourselves quite naturally, the same as that first time: we three older ones on folding chairs and Beth and Ian, cross-legged on a blanket on the grass. Our chatting trailed off, and we left a little silence, feeling the lovely peace of the setting. Then Jen began.

"I know you are remembering Jay here, which is a good thought—grateful, not sad. That's a gift of spirit, from his spirit to ours, and we may need it today, to cope with the shadow that is over us—the great loss to Ian and his family."

"It seems so pointless, so wasteful," Beth put in. "Here are these two kids, young and full of life, convinced that they are deeply in love and committed to each other, as well as to the studies and careers that they plan to share. And suddenly it's over."

She shuddered. Ian put his hand in her lap; but it was Luc who spoke. "The stupidity—deadly stupidity—of that other driver—drinking too much and getting behind the wheel."

"'My thoughts are not your thoughts, nor are your ways my ways, says the LORD.'" That was Ian, speaking low, as if to himself. He went on, "God's ways are far beyond us. Far off, in an infinite, divine wisdom, all is planned. Things seemingly violent and unjust take shape; but it's only because we can't see the whole shape, that they appear unjust and violent. If we could see it all, we would know. Is that it—and is that our comfort? Must it be?"

"I think it is," Jen said, "and it may not seem like much comfort. Admittedly, what I'm venturing to think and say is about the Transcendent. As such, it may appear quite contrary to the warning that you were just recalling, Ian. Therefore, it must be put in figurative language, and provisionally. Our starting point, the rock on which we take our stand, is the conviction—a sheer conviction of faith—that God loves. Indeed, that God *is* Love—Love that is absolute, far beyond any experience of love that we can have.

"I'd like to move from that conviction to an analogy, an experience of love that we *are* able to have: that of a young child and a loving parent. The parent may, by deliberate choice, put the child through suffering. Let's say that they are caught in a situation of war, as has been happening often in our world. The parent knows that they must evacuate their home, traveling under harsh and precarious conditions, if they hope to survive. This means hardship and suffering for the child, who isn't able to understand why. My analogy is only that, an analogy—obviously simplistic as an explanation for why, in a world under God who is Love, we experience situations that are agonizingly painful."

"For me, that is too easy," Luc said. "When we are doing our best, and things go terribly wrong; when one person on whom many others depend is suddenly struck down with an inoperable brain tumor; are we to say, 'God knows. It must be for the best'? That sounds like giving up without a struggle. Sure, in the chance occurrences in life, the cards may seem to be stacked against us. But to acquiesce, to say, 'It must be God's will that makes it so'—that's too easy.

"I find that the more natural human thing is to resist. It is to challenge fate—or so-called destiny—will-of-the-gods. We may fail repeatedly. The incurable disease may, for a long time, be incurable. But we don't accept that as part of God's design."

Ian nodded vigorously. "I agree, and I'm glad you put it that way. I certainly am not prepared, when confronted with some painful problem, just to bow my head and say, 'God's will be done.' In a world full of injustice, where even natural forces seem to favor some and leave others pitifully exposed, I'm not willing to shrug, and say, 'That's how it is; that's how it must be meant to be.'

"At the same time, I'm going to recognize that my view is limited. I live in, and am part of, this space/time universe, which is my boundary. By God's grace, my spirit reaches beyond. Spirit moves us all to be aware that we need to strive to make things just and good in this world—good for all people—while we also hold, by strong faith, to an awareness of spiritual reality that transcends what we see and know, and that gives it ultimate meaning."

Jen said. "Hold onto that, Ian. The two viewpoints need to be seen in dynamic competition: moral struggle and acceptance. Trust in God but keep up the fight. That reminds me of the World War II song: 'Praise the Lord and pass the ammunition!'"

We chuckled. Luc stood up looking at the pond and said, "I think I can still find a stone to skip."

In a moment he did find one, and sent it skipping across the water to the other side. I joined him at the pond's edge, finding and skipping smooth, flat stones.

It was a good thing that we made a pause. We had gathered with the shadow of the tragic car crash over us, and our talk had been expectedly sober. Now we had an interval to enjoy the fresh beauty of the setting. We were there a bit later in the year than the previous time, and the daffodils were beginning to fade, but the verdure of the trees had a late-spring fullness.

After a bit, as we sat again, Jen took up her line of thought.

"There is another angle to what we were discussing, which is human culpability. The tragedy that is filling our minds was the result of one person's fatally wrong behavior; on top of which, as I understand, he alone has survived the crash that he caused."

Luc spoke up quickly. "That's a good point. Spirituality is not my thing; but a lot that happens to us is our own doing—or misdoing. I've already given my view of the other driver in the accident. When he recovers, he's got to be held criminally responsible. Granted, not every case is as clear-cut as this one. But much of the time, when things go wrong, there's someone whose greed or carelessness or plain stupidity is behind it."

"Right," Jen agreed, "and we can say that from its beginnings, a primary function of human society has been to regulate responsibility; that is, to protect the innocent and punish the guilty. That's a tall order. It seldom happens that the fault is entirely on one side, and even when it seems so, who is to decide?"

"Which is why we have laws," Luc answered, "and lawyers, judges and juries—the whole legal system, plus a police force to back it up. Society has evolved it—and keeps on evolving—to hold people responsible. Is the guilty person going to come forward, on his own, and say, 'I caused it; I'm the one who did it.'?"

Beth broke in: "Obviously not! And suppose he does confess; can that make it right? Is society going to say, 'Very well, since you admit your guilt and you're sorry, you won't be punished or suffer any consequences.'? In an inter-related world, the damage anyone does is going to affect other people—maybe affect them tragically."

"The issue of responsibility, guilt and consequences comes down to motive," I offered. "Motive, in human behavior, is the critical factor. All the time, in our world, accidents are happening—from trivial to disastrous. If the cause is carelessness, or some other type of 'human error,' there may be blame to be assigned. People who are entrusted with responsibility should be held responsible, to a point of being charged with criminal negligence. But it gets a lot more serious when deliberate malice is established, an intention to cause harm in whatever way."

"And that means punishment," Jen said. "In a family, when one child hurts another, a parent steps in. She or he must try to find out what happened and why, and, if offense is intentional, the one who did the hurting must be punished. If there was serious provocation, maybe both children deserve some punishment; but deliberate injury has to have a price."

I gave an illustration. "In the history of Western civilization, Hammurabi's Babylonian code, created early in the second millennium BCE, is famous as a pioneering legal outline. Among its nearly three hundred laws are those prescribing that an injury is to be compensated by doing the same harm to the one who caused it. Later, in the Hebrew scriptures the principle is referred to as 'an eye for an eye and a tooth for a tooth.' This simple, violent code was intended to establish equal treatment under law, as well as a strong deterrent to anyone inclined to injure another. Law in a modern society has to be a lot more complex; but I'd say that the root ideas of equal treatment, compensation, and deterrence remain as a foundation."

Ian responded, "That's well and good. We'll agree that the other driver in this case, so totally at fault that it seems wrong to call it an accident, even though it wasn't a deliberate act of malice—we'll agree that he should and must be punished. He took two lives. So the law should take his life?"

"Logically, it should," Luc said. "He wasn't acting deliberately. His brain was too clouded for any deliberate action. But it was his choice that made it that way, and that then took the fatal chance of getting out on the highway. All of that, he chose to do."

"We know there's no issue of capital punishment here." That was Jen's rejoinder, and she went on. "In some societies there could be, even today. In ours, there may be a trial, as I believe there should be, and there should be a severe punishment, including considerable time in prison. It has to be made plain that, even though there was no malice, no intention, he was entirely culpable. Society should accept no excuse, and anyone else inclined to drink too much and then drive a motor vehicle should know that he or she will get the same kind of punishment for such a consequence.

"But let's think a bit more about this tragic event. Let's turn from the drunk driver back to these two young people, whom I didn't know but feel close to because of Ian."

Jen paused. I felt, as I think others did, that in that quiet place, full of springtime and the resurgence of life, there was a message that needed to be spoken.

After a moment's silence, I began. "Two physical lives were snuffed out. It was an abhorrent moment. The finality, though, is in our perspective of our space/time world, our present existence. These are two spirits. They felt, we've been told, that they were deeply in love. They were very young, but were sure that they wanted always to be together. Perhaps that actually is how it is. We can't know for now, because 'now' is how it is for us, in this place and time. They, as we believe, are not in space and time. Theirs is true and ultimate reality, transcendent reality of spirit, of the Transcendent Spirit, God.

"We've reminded ourselves, and have always present, the message that our ways are not God's ways, nor our thoughts God's thoughts. So we'll press as close as we can to the boundary, while we're aware that it is our boundary, our limit. We won't—because we can't—say how it is with these two spirits, nor with any others. We are here—in a place— now—in time. How is it, to be free of place and time—of this space/time existence? We can only trust, and hold by faith, that these two spirits—together with our spirits and all spirits—are held in the being and love of transcendent Being and Love—of God."

I stopped. There was stillness, the full-of-life stillness of that lovely place and time.

"Yes," Ian said, the one most affected. "Yes, that is where I stand, too. That's enough, for our where and when—for this present life." He seemed about to go on; then closed his lips. Beth put her arm around him, where they sat on the blanket. Then he stood, taking her hands in his to help her up.

There seemed to be a benediction about the place, as we left it, and I took a last look back at the peaceful pond among its trees.

Dialogue VI

Beth and Ian were married. It was a lovely, late-June wedding. They'd planned it for two weeks earlier and had sent out the invitations, when Alice, Ian's sister, was killed in the car crash. Beth thought they should put it off until the fall, but Ian said, No, his parents wanted them to go ahead.

The wedding was outdoors, in late afternoon, under an azure sky. There'd been a brief, quite heavy shower; but that had cleared away. For a venue, they had chosen the historic Anthony Wayne House in Westchester, a few miles west of Philadelphia. The deep lawn was damp underfoot, and some drops still glistened on low branches; but rich western sunlight flooded the whole scene as I first saw it. When I came up the walk to Wayne House, hearing the buzz of guests already there, my mind went back to last fall, to the party at Luc's house, and my hesitation to go in, remembering Jay, whom we had lost only weeks before.

The wedding was simple and beautiful—tastefully and meaningfully planned—as I expected it to be. Although Beth and Ian both had fulltime jobs, they arranged for a honeymoon week in Istanbul. They were both intrigued by the romance of the Bosporus, the meeting place of East and West, particularly as represented by the ancient and magnificent sixth century cathedral, Hagia Sofia, later a mosque and now including a museum. Ian had read the Quran, in a good translation, and several books on Islamic history and culture. So they decided on a new experience to share at the beginning of their new life together.

Our dialogue group planned to meet a month or so after Ian and Beth returned and settled into their new home. In fact, it was Beth's idea that we should gather right there. They had bought a restored row house in Philadelphia, in the Fishtown section, a "gentrified" neighborhood popular with the younger set. The living room was small, Beth said, but had a high ceiling, and windows overlooking their quiet street. We would have room enough to sit and talk in a tranquil space.

We were to meet there on Sunday afternoon, August 13th. Everyone knows what happened on Independence Mall in Philadelphia three days earlier, on Thursday, August tenth, the patriotic ceremony; a crowd gathered, including families and friends, to honor the three Navy SEALs from Philadelphia who died in the mission in Iraq that killed the top IS commander and captured two others. Television showed the heavy van that broke through a police barricade, racing right into the crowd—the footage edited, because it was too horrible to watch.

The news coverage kept on, at intervals, all evening. There was one early clip of an injured child lying by a broken folding chair, and a woman, hair mostly white, bending over, quickly lifting her, finding pressure points to stop her bleeding. I thought right away that there was something familiar about that woman, the curve of her shoulder and back of her head. In the coverage, an ABC reporter located the white-haired woman as she was leaving the scene and interviewed her briefly, face-to-face.

It was Jen! The front of her dress was stained with blood. Medics were saying that her quick action to check torn arteries may have saved the child's life. How had she known what to do?

Jen said calmly to the reporter: "I was with the Peace Corps years ago in Zaire—now the Democratic Republic of Congo. They gave us training in emergency triage."

The reporter wanted to know more, including any relationship Jen had with the SEALs who were being honored.

"No, none at all—only deep respect."

I called Jen on Friday to tell her I had seen the news clip. I expressed my admiration and said that we could postpone our scheduled dialogue. She replied that although the event had left her shaken, she felt that we ought to go ahead and meet. There were things we should talk about.

Like the previous time, at the pond—although for a different reason—we were rather subdued as we met. It was our first time with Ian and Beth as a married couple, and in their new home. We offered positive comments and congratulations, but the enthusiasm was tempered. Our hosts showed us proudly through the house, and then we sat in the living room in our familiar circle. Roland was there, of course, but with only moderate wagging of his tail, as if sensing the subdued mood.

When we were ready, Jen began. "The happening on Thursday is at the forefront of our thoughts. I'm glad we have gathered today, because I have ideas that I need to share and think through, as, probably, the rest of you do, too."

She paused, and Luc spoke up. "I think there are some details of the incident that have come to light, that should be looked at. We know that the so-called Islamic State immediately claimed responsibility, on their web site, but we don't know yet if what they said is true. Both local and national authorities will need time for investigation. As of now, no one is even sure that this terrorist acted alone, or if he was an IS terrorist as they claim. There was planning; but one obsessed individual can plan. That van appeared to be a simple delivery vehicle, and he was dressed in a work uniform; although we read that inspection of the wreck showed that the driver had rigged a weight that he could shift onto the accelerator pedal and a sort of harness to hold the steering wheel. He knew he'd likely be shot, but made sure that the van would plough right on ahead, on the course he would set. In effect, the national guards at the event, with their assault rifles at the ready, shattered the windshield and the driver with a hail of bullets, but the van kept on coming even faster, crashing into the crowd. You were there, Jen. You saw it."

Jen nodded as a grim expression crossed her face.

"What is it?" Beth asked. "What can possibly induce a person to commit such violence—indiscriminately, it seems, just trying to hurt and kill as many people as he can—and throwing away his own life to do it?"

"It's hate," I said, "fanatical hate. We've talked before about love—what a mystical power it can be in our relationships. Its obverse is hate. There are close to a thousand documented hate groups here in the United States, right now. They have various origins and various goals, but generally they hold together by vilifying and scapegoating a common enemy or enemies in society. We all know something about the Ku Klux Klan. The Southern Poverty Law Center has compiled a mass of deeply disturbing information about hate groups in America."

"No doubt about that," Luc said. "I've seen some of the facts and figures in their annual reports."

Ian spoke up. "Hate, as you said, Don, is the obverse of love. Either one has to have a person or people as its object. We can talk about love or hate in the abstract—love of country, hate of an enemy—but for the emotion to be felt it has to focus on an actual person or group of people. Some leaders are skilled at radicalizing people, particularly young people, and they make sophisticated use of social media to do so."

Beth responded: "I'd say that people who purvey hate start with other people's dissatisfaction, if not downright anger. They target individuals who are not at ease in society, who may feel shut out in some way, or left behind. Then the hatemongers set out to convince these dissatisfied people that they can become part of a new order in which they will find vindication, fulfillment, their true worth. This approach often seems to resonate with the 'lone wolf,' the solitary person in whom a well of alienation can be deep."

"On top of all of that," I said, "there can be a religious, or quasi-religious, appeal. Here IS may use isolated and distorted texts from the Quran. The KKK type of movement takes texts from the Bible. And this may bring in a perspective of afterlife, an assurance of a heavenly reward."

"How else can they get young, presumably rational men and women to strap on suicide belts loaded with explosives, and purposefully blow themselves to bits?" That was Luc's ironic comment.

Beth said, "But what about all the mass shootings in schools and shopping places by people with no apparent religious or political motive? I find it frightening—almost terrifying—to look inside a twisted human spirit and see such powerful compulsions. And I think there is an additional element, one that maybe we picked up on the long road of our evolutionary development. It's sadism. I don't like to acknowledge it; but it seems to be there.

"Take the fact that some children torture animals. Some adults also do that, and they torture other people. There seems to be, deep in our nature, a sadistic satisfaction—I don't want to say pleasure—in witnessing pain. Medieval acts of public torture, such as burnings at the stake, drew large crowds; and I don't believe it was just out of religious fervor. We've got some very dark corners in our human spirit."

That left a silence that lasted for some long moments. We heard a happy child in the street call, "Daddy, Daddy," as she seemed to be welcoming her father home.

Then Luc spoke. "The authorities are, of course, investigating exhaustively whether there were any accomplices in Thursday's criminal act. So far it seems that this van driver was a homegrown terrorist and that he acted alone. We all know from the news media that the authorities have found evidence on the suspect's device that he watched and listened to extremist propaganda. That's the cyber world we live in. People of extremist ideas can reach into corners all over the globe to find other people who can be incited to commit the violence that they want to see. How do you defend against that?"

"Security measures can be taken," Jen said. "The public can be urged to remain alert and to report immediately any suspicious object or action; but that is only haphazard, at best. National and regional security can compile and keep current their lists and data on individuals who may, for whatever reason, appear suspicious, but in our free society it's impossible to carry out surveillance to a high degree. Privacy issues aside, to employ enough undercover agents and give them the means to monitor, 24/7, the movements and contacts of even a modest list of high-profile suspects would mean person-power and expense beyond the budget and ability of any local community or of the federal government. So as far as vigilance is concerned, we can only try our best to be watchful.

"What counts for more, I'd say, are efforts at prevention, although they, too, offer no guarantees. We can try to be a more compassionate society, reaching out to people who may feel isolated, marginalized or without hope or purpose. We need to do it, not in a condescending, but an inclusive way."

"Jen," I said, "those measures are good, and we see them and applaud them in many communities. But more to the point is to identify the instigators of fanaticism, hatred and incitement to mass violence. On the internet, free speech should not be equated with a completely unregulated space to access people on a massive scale. What's more, it's at very little cost, with no attribution or responsibility. We love our free press, but we have standards of good journalism, don't we? Let's apply them to the electronic media."

Beth added, "I wonder if the promotion of violence and hatred is similar to the promotion of addictive drugs. The person who is vulnerable becomes addicted. But the responsibility for promoting addiction is where the prevention and enforcement efforts need to be placed."

"What haunts us," I said, "as in the tragic instance at the front of our minds today, is the lone wolf, the seemingly ordinary person lost in the crowd. The social media give him—and, as we've noted, it could be her—easy access to dangerous propaganda. Its focus is on the enemy—likely to be the government, as represented by the police, the military, anyone in uniform. The event on Independence Mall presented an obvious target. Violence, as much violence as possible, would be revenge, and loss of his own life in carrying it out would be vindication."

Luc responded, "So, how do you combat that extremism? Do you say, 'We'll wipe out all of these extremists. We'll track them down, one by one, and take them out'?"

"Of course that's impossible," Jen said. "They are too many and too widely scattered. Besides, radical movements can rarely be snuffed out by that kind of force. Think of the imperial power of Ancient Rome and the early Christian movement. When Rome's emperor declared the nascent

Christian community to be subversive, he resolved to stamp it out by force; but repressive measures—even brutal public executions—seemed only to galvanize the new faith and bring more converts. As a later saying put it: 'The blood of martyrs is the seed of the church.'"

Ian said, "We'll agree that similar groups of murderous fanatics are going to spring up for each one that is eliminated. But hunting down and bringing to justice any terrorists who survive their plots has to be done.

"At the same time, it must be made clear, anywhere in the world, that violent civil, quasi-religious movements will not be allowed. All free nations, whatever their religious heritage, need to be brought together on this urgent issue."

There was silence. We all seemed busy with our thoughts, pondering them against the background of the week's horrific event that had occurred so near to where we were sitting.

Then Jen spoke. "Ian, I'd say that you've brought to a conclusion our dialogue of today, as well as larger thoughts on hate and love."

"Then it's time," Beth said brightly, "to relax with something more congenial. I've made a casserole of enchiladas, remembering a long-ago specialty of my mom, and rice and salad, and we have beer—or wine, for any who prefer it."

In no time, with Ian's help, the dining table was set and we were gathered around it, savoring Beth's enchiladas and the fixings.

When the supper was finished and the plates cleared I retrieved from the kitchen five flutes, as well as two bottles of champagne I'd left chilling in the refrigerator.

Setting out the flutes, I opened and poured the champagne, then stood to say, "I'd like to propose a toast: to Jen, whose wisdom, tact, and graciousness have lent invaluable leadership to us in our dialogues of these past months."

We drank to that, and then Jen stood to respond: "And I offer a toast to Beth and Ian, our kind hosts. May your life together be long and full of happiness—for you and for all whose lives you brighten."

That toast, also, we drank with full hearts. Now Luc stood and added a mention that surprised me:

"I give you, in a toast, my friend Don. Our friendship, begun those thirty years ago when we were a pair of graduate students on vacation, undertaking to build a log cabin in New Hampshire, has blossomed in the year and more that you've been here, Don, in our community. Don has told me that he'll be leaving soon, returning to Augusta, Georgia, to a position he's been offered there. So here's to you, Don, to our friendship, that I prize more than ever—and, may I add, here's to our dialogue group, for what it has meant to me."

It was hard to break up that day. We promised—I, particularly—that we would keep in touch. As we stood on the front steps of Ian and Beth's home, I felt our spirits embracing, held in the transcendent Spirit. So may it continue, whatever should come to each one in this world of space and time.

Other works by Donald R. Fletcher:

I, Lucas, Wrote the Book, Xlibris, 2003
(an imaginative recreation of the writing of the Third Gospel)

View From the Playroom Floor, Xlibris, 2004
(contemporary philosophical/theological reflections)

Turnings: Lyric Poems Along a Road, Outskirts Press, 2009
(a combined memoir and anthology of personal poems)

The Gift: Looking to Jesus As He Was, CreateSpace, 2010
(an analytical study of historical traces of Jesus in the Gospels)

Martha and I: Life, Love and Loss in Alzheimer's Shadow,
Wipf and Stock Publishers, 2017 (republished)
(an account of the long struggle with the author's wife's illness, combined with scenes of her as she was throughout her earlier life)

By Scalpel and Cross: A Missionary Doctor in Old Korea,
Resource Publications, Wipf and Stock Publishers, 2016
(the story of a Presbyterian medical missionary told against the background of Korea in the first half of the twentieth century)

Dialogues with Jay: On Life and Afterlife, Resource Publications, Wipf and Stock Publishers, 2017
(patterned roughly after Plato, dialogues of five people sharing their thoughts on an afterlife beyond the boundaries of space and time)